Teen ELI Readers

W0288547

The ELI Readers collection is a complete range of books and plays for readers of all ages, ranging from captivating contemporary stories to timeless classics. There are four series, each catering for a different age group; First ELI Readers, Young ELI Readers, Teen ELI Readers and Young Adult ELI Readers. The books are carefully edited and beautifully illustrated to capture the essence of the stories and plots.

FSC
www.fsc.org
MIX
Paper from responsible sources
FSC® C127663

The FSC® certification guarantees that the paper used in these publications comes from certified forests, promoting responsible forestry management worldwide.

ECO-LIBRIS
www.ecolibris.net

For this series of ELI graded readers, we have planted 5000 new trees.

Dear Diary...

A Collection of the World's Best Diaries

Edited by Liz Ferretti
Illustrated by Francesca Capellini

Teen ELi Readers

Dear Diary…
A Collection of the World's Best Diaries
Edited by Elizabeth Ferretti
Language Level Consultants Janet Borsbey and Ruth Swan
Illustrated by Francesca Capellini

ELI Readers
Founder and Series Editors
Paola Accattoli, Grazia Ancillani, Daniele Garbuglia (Art Director)

Graphic Design
Airone Comunicazione, Sergio Elisei

Layout
Airone Comunicazione, Diletta Brutti

Production Manager
Francesco Capitano

Bibliography
Hedi Kole, *The Subway Diaries*, Bohemian Therapy Publishing LLC (2009).
Bob Dylan, *Chronicles Volume One*, Pocket Books (2005) (An imprint of Simon and Schuster UK Ltd).
Kurt Cobain, *Kurt Cobain Journals*, Penguin Books (2003).
Salvador Dalí, *Diary of a Genius*, Hutchinson & Co (1966).
Frida Kahlo, *The Diary of Frida Kahlo. An Intimate Self-Portrait*, Bloomsbury (1995).
Andy Warhol, *The Andy Warhol Diaries*, Simon and Schuster (1989).
Adam Plummer, *Slave Diaries*, http://anacostia.si.edu/Plummer/Plummer_Diary.htm
Anne Frank, *The Diary of A Young Girl*, Simon and Schuster (1989).
Zlata Filipović , *Zlata's Diary. A Child's Life in Sarajevo*, Puffin Books (1995).
The Freedom Writers, with Erin Gruwell, *The Freedom Writers Diary*, Broadway Books (2009).
Ralph Waldo Emerson, *Emerson In His Journals, selected and edited by Joel Porte, Journals and Miscellaneous Notebooks of Ralph Waldo Emerson, Volume X: 1847-1848*, (Harvard University Press).
Louisa May Alcott, *Louisa May Alcott, Her Life Letters and Journals. Edited by Ednah D. Cheney.*
Virginia Woolf, *The Diary of Virginia Woolf Volume IV 1931-1935*, The Hogarth Press (1982).
George Orwell, *The Orwell Diaries*, Penguin Modern Classics (2010).
Charles Darwin, *Charles Darwin's Diary of the Voyage of H.M.S. "Beagle"*.
Ernesto 'Che' Guevara, *The Motorcycle Diaries*, Harper Perennial (2004)
David Byrne, *The Bicycle Diaries*, Faber and Faber (2009).
Helen Fielding, *Bridget Jones's Diary*, Picador (1997).
Jeff Kinney, *The Diary of a Wimpy Kid*, Puffin (2007).

Extracts from the publications listed in the bibliography have been simplified to aid comprehension.

Photo credits
Getty Images, Olycom, Shutterstock

New edition 2021
First edition 2014
© ELI s.r.l.
P.O. Box 6
62019 Recanati MC
Italy
T +39 071750701
F +39 071977851
info@elionline.com
www.elionline.com

Typeset in 13 / 18 pt Monotype Dante
Printed in Italy by Tecnostampa Recanati – ERT 234.10
ISBN 978-88-536-3197-8

www.eligradedreaders.com

CONTENTS

These icons indicate the parts of the text that are recorded

start ▶ **stop** ■

Introduction

This book is a collection* of some of the world's best diaries. Here you will find writers, artists, thinkers and musicians, children and young people, who tell us about their lives.

Your Best Friend

Diaries can change people's lives. In this book, you will meet two young girls who find themselves in the middle of war. Their diaries become their best friends. Writing a diary helps them to never lose hope, even when their lives are in danger. Later, their stories will help some young people in America to change *their* lives.

Real Lives

When we read these diaries we can find out who the diary writer really was, not who we think they were. It is as if they are talking to us. We begin to understand that they are not only famous, but real people.

collection a group of things kept together

Secret* Spaces

Diaries are the place where we can write our thoughts, and they can help us understand our problems. The things we write don't always seem important at the time, but later, we see how we, and our ideas, have changed. Diaries are a great way to remember the little details that make our lives special.

Online Diaries

The people in this book wrote their diaries on paper. Today, we have online diaries. Here, we can write about our day, but also add photographs, and pictures – anything we choose. This can bring a diary to life. The best thing is, no one else can read it but you!

Diaries are fun to keep, they can be a great way to practise a foreign language, and they can help you become a better writer.

secret something that only you know

Chapter 1

Musicians' Diaries

HEIDI KOLE

▶ 2 Heidi Kole is a musician. *The Subway* Diaries* is the story of how Heidi started playing her songs in the New York subway in early 2006. *The Subway Diaries* shows us what life under the streets of New York is like.

Heidi was a singer and a dancer, she was also a stunt woman* in films. Then she had a bad accident, and was in so much pain that she couldn't work. She had an idea for earning money, but she wasn't sure if she could do it...

Heidi Kole in the New York City subway

Monday January 16th, 2006

It was cold ... I can't tell you how many times I wanted to turn round and go back home. But with my guitar on my back, I entered the subway station. I had no idea where to go. The New York City subways have one hundred stations, and carry five million people a day.

stunt woman/man person who does the dangerous things in films
subway (American English) trains that go under the city

Heidi Kole, and many subway musicians around the world, often have problems because the police want them to stop playing. Heidi says that's wrong, she says subway musicians make people's lives better. What do you think?

Friday January 19th, 2007

Our music makes people dance, clap*, move, and they give us some money and look happy. From what I have seen in my years underground*, we are probably the happiest workers in New York City.

In 2008, Heidi was able to join MUNY (Music Under New York). She was now an official subway musician. That meant she wouldn't have so many problems with the police.

Playing music in the streets or the subway, to earn money from people, is called busking. Street musicians are called buskers.

A New York City subway train

clap hit your hands together
underground under the city

BOB DYLAN

born 1941

3 Bob Dylan was born Robert Allen Zimmerman in 1941. This American singer-songwriter first became famous during the 60s.

Bob Dylan published *Chronicles Volume 1*, in 2004. In this book he tells the story of his life. We read how he becomes a musician, and about the musicians he saw as his teachers.

Chapter 2. Why I Write

I don't know when I had the idea to write my own songs. I think it happens slowly. You don't wake up one day and decide that you need to write songs. It's not that easy. You want to write songs that are bigger than life.

Two of Bob Dylan's most famous songs, *Blowing in the Wind* and *The Times they are a-Changin'*, talk about the problems of being black in the US during segregation*.

segregation time in American history (to 1964) when black children could not go to "white" schools, etc.

In *Chronicles*, we learn how much Bob Dylan hated being famous. He didn't feel he was the "voice of a generation*" that everyone called him. For Bob, it was important to remember that famous people are real people.

Chapter 3. New Morning

I had a wife and children who I loved more than anything. I was just trying to make enough money, but the press* kept saying I was the voice of a generation. That was funny. Being true to yourself was more important to me than all that.

I'm Not There (2007) is a film about Bob Dylan. Dylan is played by six different actors.

Bob Dylan has written music all his life, and he still gives concerts around the world. His music comes from the music traditions* of America and Europe.

voice of a generation person who speaks for people who are the same age as he/she is

press TV, radio, newspapers

traditions ideas and way of life, from the past to the present

4 Kurt Cobain was the singer in the band Nirvana. Nirvana became famous in the late 1980s and early 1990s.

Kurt Cobain's diary is full of drawings, ideas for songs, and his thoughts about life. Here, he describes how he feels about being in a band.

You can make money, but it's not a good job to choose. I feel everyone is looking at me twenty-four hours a day. Being in a band is hard work, and being famous itself isn't enough – except if you still like playing, and I do. I love playing live.

Nirvana's most famous song *Smells Like Teen Spirit*, comes from their 1991 album *Nevermind*.

Like Bob Dylan, Kurt Cobain found being famous difficult. He thought that people didn't understand him.

He was also called "the voice of a generation", and he was unhappy with that.

KURT COBAIN

1967 - 1994

Kurt Cobain often thought about what people wrote about him and his band. He got more and more tired of the press saying things that were not true.

Music journalists* are paid to find interesting little stories about a musician. If there isn't enough to write about, they have to spice* it up. If it still isn't spicy enough, which is almost always what happens, then the editor* puts in more spice. The editor's job is to sell magazines.

Kurt Cobain had very bad problems in the last years of his life. He had depression*, and began to find his life too difficult. He died when he was only 27 years old.

Nirvana played a new kind of punk rock. Their type of music is called Grunge, and was very popular in the 1990s.

OH OUR LAST AND FINAL NAME IS **NIRVANA** ooh eerie mystical Doom

depression feeling so unhappy that you become ill
editor person who decides what goes in a newspaper
journalist person who writes for newspapers
spice (here) make something more interesting/exciting

Artists' Pages

SALVADOR DALÍ

1904 - 1989

5 Salvador Dalí was a Spanish Surrealist artist – he did not paint things as they are, but as he felt about them. His work often looks as if it has come from a bad dream. For example, three clocks in his most famous work look soft, not hard.

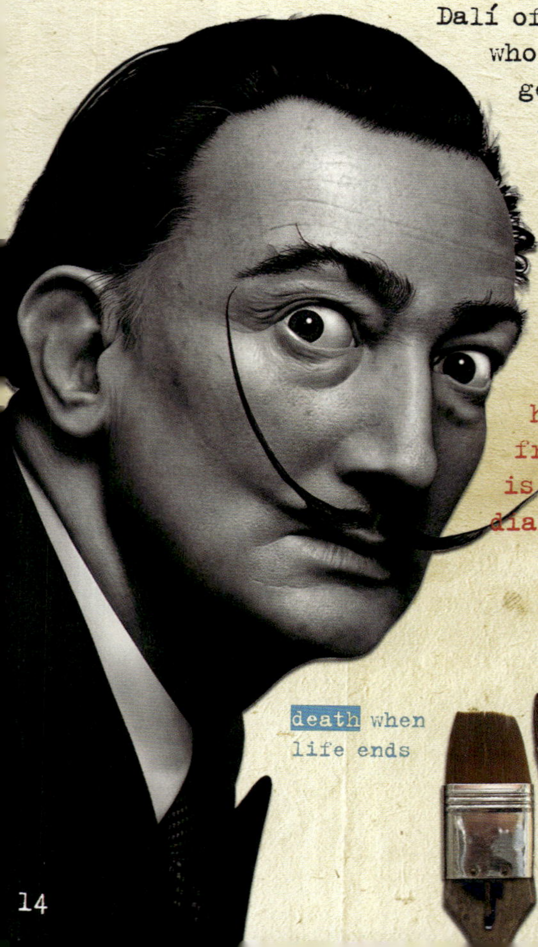

Dalí often said he was a special person, who could do amazing things – a genius. His second published diary is called *Diary of a Genius*! It describes his life between 1952 and 1963.

This book will show that the daily life of a genius, his sleep, what he eats, his happy times, his hands, his colds, his body, his life and death* are different from all other people. This book is special, because it is the first diary written by a genius.

Does Dalí believe he is special, or is he making fun of our ideas about genius?

death when life ends

Salvador Dalí was a strong person. He liked to wear strange clothes, and people were often surprised at what he did and said.

In this extract*, Dalí tells us about a time when he forgot to do something. Photographers and journalists are waiting, but...

September 1958
I completely forgot that I had to show the world my new idea for a pretty bottle. Everyone was waiting. I quickly took a flash bulb* from a photographer. 'Here is my idea,' I said. 'It's not a drawing!' someone said. 'No,' I answered, 'it's much better.'

Dalí is often described as crazy or strange. Today, he is seen as an important artist, and his diary is full of interesting, funny ideas – like his idea to use a flashbulb as a bottle.

extract short piece of writing
flash bulb makes a strong light when you take a photo

FRIDA KAHLO

▶ 6 Frida Kahlo was a Mexican painter. She became famous for the many paintings she did of herself. The culture* of Mexico was important to her. She used bright colours and often wore traditional Mexican clothes.

Frida's diary is an artist's diary, full of drawings, colour and words. Here, Frida describes something she remembers from when she was six years old.

I had an imaginary* friend – a little girl. I used to draw a "door" on the window in my bedroom with my finger. I often went through the door, where my friend waited for me. I don't remember what she looked like, but I remember that she laughed a lot.

Frida Kahlo had a bad accident when she was young, and had to spend a lot of time in bed. This is when she started painting.

culture how people live in a country
imaginary not real

Frida kept her diary for the last ten years of her life. These were difficult years. She was often ill and spent a lot of time in hospital. At the end of the diary, Frida writes about her family.

April 1954
My father was a sick man, but I was a very happy child. He was kind and hard-working (he was a photographer and a painter). He understood my problems, like when I was four and I saw a terrible fight* between the Mexican rebels* and the army*.

Frida Kahlo only became internationally famous for her art in the 1980s, forty years after she died. During the 1980s, people started to see her work outside Mexico and, in 2002, a film was made of her life. In 2005, many of her works were shown at the Tate Modern, in London. One year later, one of her paintings was sold for several million dollars.

army large number of men who go to war for their country
fight (here) when people try to hurt or kill each other
rebels people who use war to change their country

The Casa Azul – the Blue House where Frida lived with her husband Diego Rivera, who was also a famous Mexican artist.

1928 - 1987

7 Andy Warhol was an American artist, writer, photographer and film maker. He is an important person in American culture. His first job was to draw advertisements; he became an artist in the 1950s. His most famous works show cans of soup, and he painted portraits* of famous people like Marilyn Monroe and Elvis Presley.

Andy Warhol's Diaries start in 1976 and end with his death in 1987. Every morning, Andy Warhol spoke to his secretary, Pat Hackett, on the phone. He told her everything that had happened the day before, and Pat wrote it down.

Warhol's famous portrait of Marilyn Monroe

Sunday November 28th 1976
It was a beautiful day. We walked over to the Pierre Hotel to meet Jodie Foster*. Said hello to a lot of people who said hello to me. At the hotel I saw a beautiful woman looking at me. It was Ingrid Bergman*.

Andy Warhol loved being with famous people (often called *celebrities* in English).
In his diaries, he always talks about the many celebrities that he knows.

Ingrid Bergman from Sweden, in *Casablanca* with Humphrey Bogart
Jodie Foster in *Taxi Driver*, *The Silence of the Lambs*, also makes her own films
portrait picture (usually of a person)

ANDY WARHOL

Andy Warhol

In this extract, Andy Warhol goes to a birthday party for a popular American cookie*. He wants to paint a portrait of the cookie, and he hopes that someone will pay him to do it.

Friday June 6th 1986

There was a dinner for the Oreo cookie.

I really want to do the cookie's portrait. It's having its seventy-fifth birthday. I was dressed in black and white, so I looked like an Oreo. When the cameras were on, I ate the cookies and said, 'Miss Oreo wants me to paint her portrait.'

Andy Warhol's paintings are some of the most expensive in the world. *Eight Elvises* was sold in 2008 for $100 million.

Andy Warhol often wore big glasses and had silver hair. He said "In the future, everyone will be world-famous for fifteen minutes."

cookie sweet, dry cake

True Stories

slave man, woman or child who 'belongs to' another person

ADAM F. PLUMMER

1819 - 1905

8 Adam Francis Plummer was born in 1819 in Maryland, America. He started writing his diary in 1841, after he married Emily Arnold. He wrote his diary until he died in 1905. This writer was a slave*, and this is one of the only diaries that was written by a slave.

Adam Plummer didn't write much in his diary, often just the dates of when people died, but in this extract, we read something terrible.

My wife, Emily Plummer, and four of our children were sold, on November 25th, 1851. She was bought by Mrs. M. A. Thompson in Washington City. There she stayed for a short time. About four years passed, and I did not see her once. In 1855, I wrote several letters to see or hear from her, but I did not hear from her.

Slaves could not learn to read and write, so Adam Plummer had to learn without telling anyone. Here, Adam writes that his daughter was sold.

Miss Sarah Miranda Plummer of Georgetown, sold to New Orleans, on Napoleon Avenue.

Fortunately, this story has a happy ending. After many years, the family was together again. Adam worked as a slave on a large farm in Maryland. In 1864, slaves in Maryland were free. After that, Adam was given a good job at the farm – he was able to save money, and bought a place to build a house for his family.

Hyattsville, July 14th 1868

Received from Adam Plummer three hundred and forty-four dollars and seventy five cents, for a place to build a house. Sold to him this day.

Dear Father bought hundreds of pretty flowers for our home, and other expensive plants and trees. (Written by Adam's daughter, Nellie Plummer).

1929 - 1945

ANNE FRANK

Anne Frank in May 1942

9 Anne Frank was born in Frankfurt-am-Main, Germany. Her family were Jews*, so, in 1933, they moved to Amsterdam to leave the dangers of Hitler's Germany.

Anne was given a red and white diary as a present on her thirteenth birthday. Only a few weeks later, the German army arrived in Holland. Anne and her family had to hide* in secret rooms.

Wednesday 8th July 1942
I knew this was my last night in my own bed, but I slept immediately and didn't wake until Mummy called me at 5.30 the next morning the house wasn't tidy, but it wasn't important. We only wanted to get away, escape*, and stay safe.

In her famous diary, Anne writes about what it is like to hide, worried that someone will find her and her family.

escape run from danger
hide go where no one can find you
Jews group of people who came from the country now called Israel

Anne couldn't always talk to her family about how she was feeling. Her diary became her best friend.

In their secret rooms, Anne and her family had a radio, and they knew what was happening to other Jews.

Saturday 15th July 1944
I am surprised to find that I still believe people are good at heart*. I cannot live a life built on bad things. I see terrible things happening in this world, but when I look up at the sky, I feel that everything will be better one day.

Anne's red and white diary

The house in Amsterdam where Anne and her family hid

The German police found Anne and her family on 4th August 1944. Anne and her sister died in Bergen-Belsen in March 1945. Anne was 15. Anne's father, Otto, did not die in the war. He decided to publish* his daughter's diary, so the world could know what happened to her.

good at heart good inside
publish make a book that people can buy

ZLATA FILIPOVI

A Child's Li

10 Zlata Filipović was born in 1980. Zlata started keeping a diary in 1991. She was living with her fami in Sarajevo, in Bosnia and Herzegovina, when the Bosnian War started in 1992.

Zlata's Diary tells us about life in a city that is in the middle of a war. It was a horrible time and people were afraid. It was difficult for the family to find food or water. They were very worried about what would happen, and death was everywhere.

April 5th, 1992

I'm trying to do my homework, but I can't. Something is happening in town. You can hear the war outside the city. A lot of people are coming from Dobrinja*. They're trying to stop something, but they don't know what.

You can feel that something is coming, something very bad.

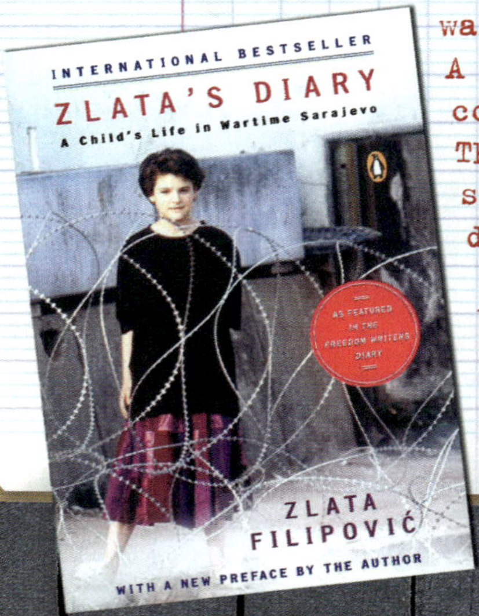

*Dobrinja part of Sarajevo

n Sarajevo

In the next extract, Zlata describes how worried she is about her mother. She has seen on the TV that some terrible things have happened on the street where her grandparents live. This is where Zlata's mother has gone.

May 27th, 1992

We went to the window, hoping to see Mummy, but she wasn't back. At 16:00, Daddy decided to go to the hospital. I looked out of the window one more time and ... SAW MUMMY RUNNING ACROSS THE BRIDGE. Thank God, Mummy is with us. Thank God.

Zlata was called the Anne Frank of Sarajevo, but Zlata's story is different from Anne's. Zlata and her family escaped from Sarajevo in 1993. They went first to the United States, then to Ireland. Zlata studied at Oxford University, and is now a writer.

New York City: commuters in subway

Nirvana

Vietnam War protestors

28th August 1963: Martin Luther King Jr (1929 – 1968) during the March on Washington after delivering his 'I Have a Dream' speech, Washington, DC.

Survivors of Auschwitz leaving the camp at the end of World War II, Poland, February 1945. Above them is the German slogan 'Arbeit macht frei' ('Work makes one free').

This image was taken during the war in 1992 in Sarajevo in the partially destroyed National Library.

FREEDOM WRITERS*

Erin Gruwell studied to be an English teacher. Her first job was at a school in Long Beach, California, where her class had a lot of "difficult" students. She soon saw that the students were like this because their lives were very difficult, and they could be hurt or killed.

Erin used writing to help her students change their lives. *The Freedom Writers Diary* was written by Erin and her students.

Autumn 1995

Hope is not a word my students use. When I asked a new student, "Do you think you will finish school?" he said, "Finish school? I don't know if I will live to be sixteen." To some of these kids, death is more real than a diploma*.

Erin decided to give her students the diaries of Anne Frank and Zlata Filipović to read. Then she asked them to write their own diaries.

Erin Gruwell

Some of the Freedom Writers

freedom being free
diploma paper to show you have finished your studies well

Writing their own diaries helped the students to understand their lives. Their teacher, Erin Gruwell, also took the time to listen to them. She helped her students meet Zlata Filipović, and other people who had lived through war and danger.

One day, they met Miep Gies, who had helped Anne Frank. This extract was written by one of Erin's students.

Spring 1996

My friend said to Miep she was a hero*. She answered, "No. You, my friends, are the true heroes." Heroes? Us? When I heard her say that I saw how special my classmates are. It feels good to know that my friends and I are doing the right thing.

Reading books and writing their own diaries, also helped Erin's students to believe in themselves. All of her students finished school, and many went to college.

In 2007, this diary became the film *Freedom Writers*.

hero wonderful person

Chapter 4

The Writer's Diary

1803 - 1882

RALPH WALDO EMERSON

12 Ralph Waldo Emerson was one of America's greatest thinkers. He believed that people should be free to think in new ways.

Emerson thought that most people are too interested in their own lives. Because of this, they don't understand how beautiful nature is.

June–July 1866

Seven men went on a walk. One was a farmer, he saw the plants; the next was an astronomer*, he saw the sky; the doctor walked and thought only of people who were ill; he was followed by a soldier*, who thought about war; then came a scientist*, he wrote everything down; after him came the estate agent*,

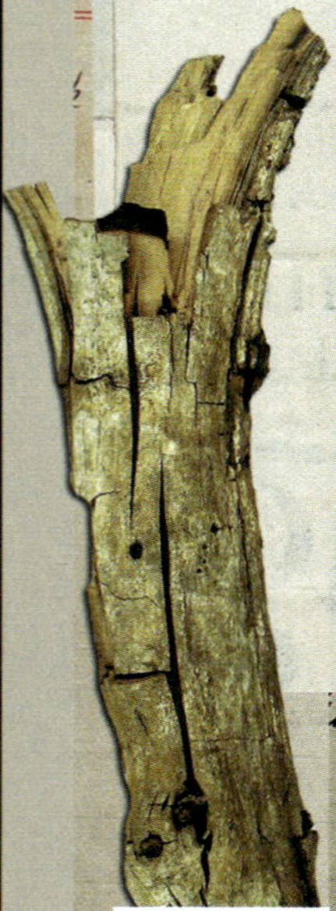

astronomer person who studies the stars
estate agent person who sells houses
scientist person who studies animals/plants/people
soldier person who goes to war

who saw how many houses he could build. The writer came and looked at the sun on the trees, and sat to listen to the music of the birds.

Ralph Waldo Emerson

Emerson believed you will never stop learning through your whole life. You can learn from nature, but also from people.

Life is the only teacher, and we get lessons from life that are better than at any school. I speak to person A and learn what he is feeling; I write about person B, and what he knows; I enjoy reading person C's great thoughts; person E comes, and says all this is wrong... My only secret was that I have learned something from everyone I have met. I never saw anyone who was not better than me at something, and I would be happy to learn from each one. ■

God in Nature
For Emerson, God was in nature and the world we see around us. He thought we can only understand God if we study nature.

1832 - 1888

13 This American writer is famous for her books *Little Women* (1868), *Little Men* (1871) and *Jo's Boys* (1886). *Little Women* tells the story of four sisters, who live in the house where Louisa and her three sisters grew up.

Louisa wrote a diary all her life. In this first extract, we see how excited she is about writing.

August 1860
I was feeling so full of ideas, that for four weeks I wrote all day and planned nearly all night. I thought of nothing except my work. I was very happy. I finished the book, and put it away for a while. Mother told Mr Emerson* about it, and he wants to read it.
I don't suppose anything will happen with it; but I had to write it, and I feel good that I have finished my first book.

Mr Emerson Ralph Waldo Emerson – a family friend

LOUISA MAY ALCOTT

Louisa got tired when she was writing. In this extract, she reads her work to her family.

February 1861

After three weeks of writing, I was very tired, and no sleep would come. So I put down the pen, and took long walks, cold baths, and played with my sister Anna. I read all I had written to my family; and Father said: "Mr Emerson must see this." Mother said it was wonderful, and Anna laughed and cried, saying, "My dear, I'm proud of* you." So I had a good time; it was wonderful to have my dear family sit up until midnight, listening with wide-open eyes to my novel*.

Louisa's diaries were made into a book called *Louisa May Alcott, Her Life Letters and Journals*. You can find it at Project Gutenberg.

novel a long story about people, written by a writer

proud of pleased with

Orchard House, Concord, Massachusetts – home of the Alcott Family, 1858

1882 - 1941

VIRGINIA WOOLF

14 Virginia Woolf was an English writer who liked to play with words and language. Her way of writing is very modern. She is most famous for her novels *Mrs Dalloway* (1925), *To the Lighthouse* (1927) and *The Waves* (1931).

Virginia wrote about her work in her diary. In this extract, she talks about how she wants to find new ways to write about things.

Virginia Woolf, at the age of 20

October 29th, 1933

I will not be "famous", or "great". I will go on in my adventure, changing, opening my mind* and my eyes. I don't want people to tell me who I am and what I can do. The thing is to free yourself: to grow and not be stopped.

Virginia Woolf was part of a big group of writers, artists and thinkers. They lived in a part of London called Bloomsbury, and so they were called the "Bloomsbury Group".

mind inside your head; where you think

A lot of sad things happened in Virginia's life. Her mother and one of her sisters died when Virginia was young, and she spent time in hospital after her father died. She had depression for many years, and took her own life in 1941.

Virginia near the end of her life

cool not hot

In this extract, Virginia describes how she feels inside. Yesterday she was ill, but today things are better.

Thursday 26th May, 1932
Today, I am surprised that my head doesn't feel so heavy. I can think, and work well. Perhaps this is the start of another good time for my writing. Yesterday, I tried to understand my depression. This morning, the inside of my head feels cool* and quiet.

Virginia Woolf believed women writers needed a place to write, and they also needed to have enough money. She talked about this in *A Room of One's Own*.

GEORGE ORWELL

POSTCARD
1903 - 1950

George Orwell was an English journalist and writer. He is most famous for his books *Nineteen Eighty-Four* (1949) and *Animal Farm* (1945). In these stories, people are not free to live as they want, and must do what they are told.

In 1936, George Orwell went on a journey to the north of England. Here he saw how poor the people were, and how hard they had to work. In this extract from his diary, he describes the black faces of the miners he met.

15 *15th March 1936*

I have seen miners* sitting down to eat with faces that are all black, except red mouths, which become clean by eating. Miners usually keep their hair short... They go to the baths, but only once a week – they don't have much time between working and sleeping.

George Orwell

miners

George Orwell kept a diary all his life. He wrote about the things that he saw every day, but also about his ideas and thoughts.

In 1938, Orwell travelled to Marrakech, in Morocco.

13th September 1938
There are so many people asking for money that it is not possible to walk through the streets. Children ask for bread, and when given it, eat it immediately and very fast. You can see many people sleeping in the street, a family in every door way... I am told they have come from the south to find food.

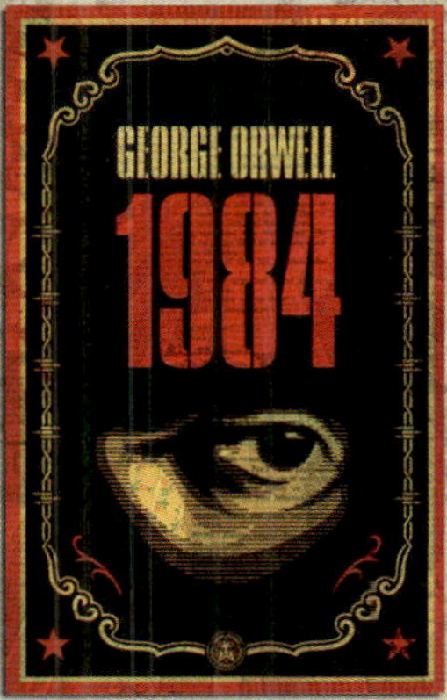

George Orwell is one of the most important English writers of the twentieth century.

George Orwell's real name was Eric Arthur Blair. He made a lot of new words that we use in English today, such as Cold War, Big Brother and thought police.

Chapter 5

Journeys

CHARLES DARWIN

1809 - 1882

16 Charles Darwin was an English scientist who said that all life changes over time. Darwin explained his ideas in *On the Origin of Species* (1859).

Between 1831 and 1836, Darwin travelled round the world on a sailing ship, called H.M.S. Beagle. He kept a diary of his journey. In this extract, he writes about what he saw on the Galápagos Islands.

September 17, 1835
The sea was full of fish, and other sea animals. They were everywhere we looked. Fishing lines were put into the water, and the men soon caught large numbers of big fish. This sport made everyone happy, and you could hear the men laughing a lot. After dinner, some of them went to the island to catch tortoises*. These islands are perfect for all types of animal.

tortoise 

lizard 

September 17, 1835

The black rocks on the island are covered in large lizards* called iguanas. They are horrible to look at. They are as black as the rocks they walk on, and get their food in the sea... I left the ship and collected ten different flowers. The birds are not afraid of us, they have never seen men before.

September 21, 1835

In my walk, I saw two very large tortoises. One was eating a plant, then he walked away. The other made a noise. They were so heavy, I couldn't lift them up. They looked as if they came from a different world.

Darwin's ideas changed the way we see our world, and helped us to understand how animals and plants change over time.

Charles Darwin

1928 - 1967

CHE GUEVARA

Che Guevara

17 Ernesto 'Che' Guevara was born in Argentina into a family with thousands of books. He studied medicine at the University of Buenos Aires. During that time, he made two important journeys, and saw the difficult lives of poor people. In 1951–1952, Che Guevara made a long journey on a motorcycle through South America, with his friend Alberto Granada. Guevara wrote about this journey in *The Motorcycle Diaries*.

The person who wrote these words died the moment his feet arrived in Argentina. The person who makes these words better, me, does not live now. What I mean is, I am not the person I was. All this travelling through 'our' America has changed me more than I thought.

Guevara saw that in many countries poor people had terrible lives. He wanted big changes to happen and thought that war was the best way to make these changes. He believed in the ideas of Karl Marx, and helped his friend Fidel Castro win a war in Cuba.

Che and Alberto didn't have much money on their journey, and didn't always have a lot to eat. In this extract they stay with a doctor friend of Alberto's.

We stopped next in Necochea. We arrived in time for lunch. We got a warm welcome from the friend, but not from his wife. "You haven't finished your studies to become a doctor, but you're going away? You have no idea when you'll be back? But why?" she asked.

During his journey, Che visited Argentina, Chile, Peru, Ecuador, Colombia, Venezuela, Panama and the US.

Today, Che Guevara is both loved and hated. He was clever, and worked to help poor people all over the world, but he believed war was the best way to make changes in the world. He was killed in Bolivia in 1967. ◘

A famous scene from the film *Little Women*, 1949.

The young Ernesto
"Che" Guevara

A BBC programme during Orwell's time.

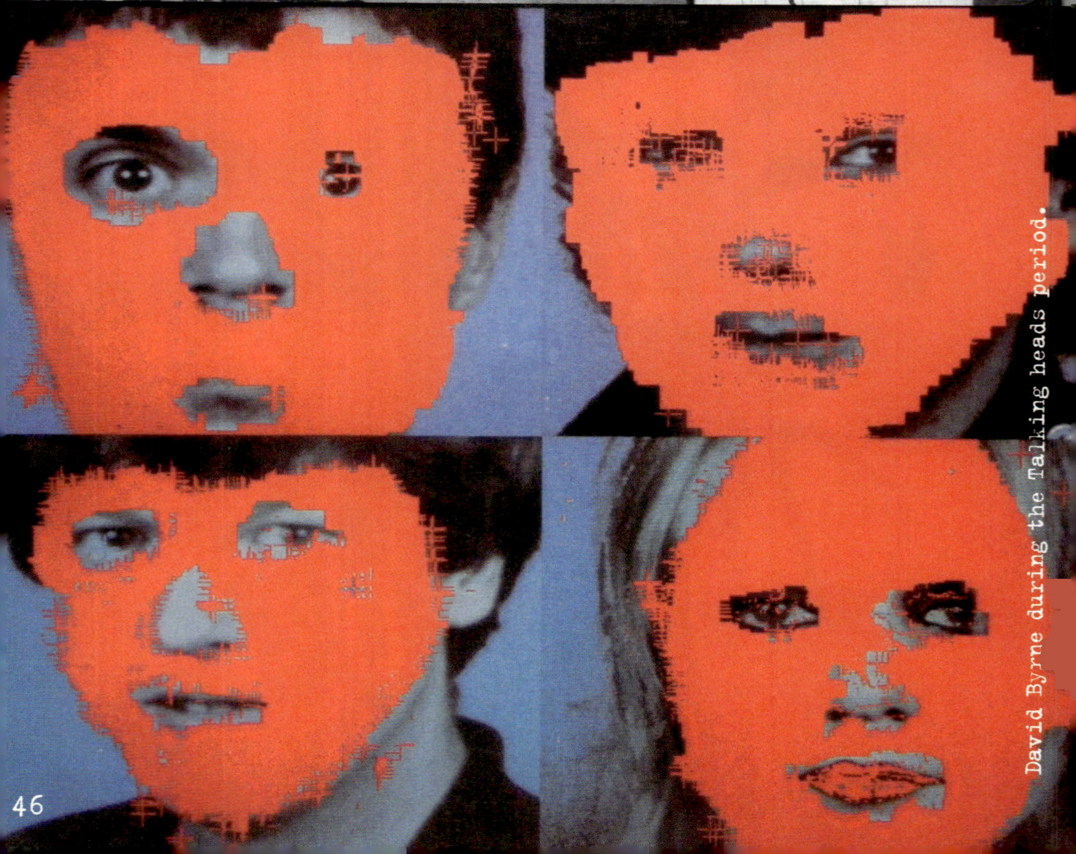

David Byrne during the Talking heads period.

Vanessa Bell (Virginia Woolf's sister),
Portrait of Lytton Strachey

18 David Byrne was in the band Talking Heads, who had several popular songs from 1975 to 1991. He still gives many concerts around the world. David Byrne has kept a diary for most of his life.

Musicians spend a lot of time waiting for their next concert. David Byrne decided to use that time to find out about the places where he was staying. He bought a folding bicycle*, which he could take everywhere. He wrote about the journeys he made on his bicycle in a diary, published as *The Bicycle Diaries* in 2009.

I felt free and happy as I cycled around many of the world's big cities. I felt closer to the life on the streets, and I could stop when I wanted. It was often faster than a car or a taxi. I felt the same in every town I went to.

folding bicycle

DAVID BYRNE

David Byrne says that some cities are easy to cycle in. Some are safe and others are more dangerous, but if you are careful, he says, all of them are interesting.

In *The Bicycle Diaries*, David describes cycling in San Francisco, New York, London, Manila... There was a lot of traffic in all of these cities, but David was always happy on his bicycle!

Ride a bike in Istanbul? Are you crazy? Yes... and no. The traffic here is crazy, but there is so much traffic that I can get round the centre of the city faster on a bike than in a car. Here, I am usually the only person on a bike.

The city of New York had a competition. They wanted new ideas for bike racks, where you can keep your bike safe if you are away from home. David Byrne helped to choose the winner.

David Byrne

Chapter 6

Diaries as Stories

19 This is a fictional* diary, written by Helen Fielding. In this funny book, Bridget Jones tells us abou her life, her family, and the men she meets. The story is like *Pride and Prejudice* by Jane Auster

Bridget is over thirty years old, and does not have boyfriend. She thinks she will never find the perfe man! She is always worried about her job, how much she is eating, and how she looks. At the start of th story, Bridget thinks she can't do anything.

I'm no good at anything. Not men. Not talking to people. Not work. Nothing.

Then things get worse! Everything she does makes things more difficult than before.

Everyone knows that when one part of your life starts going okay, another part starts going very wrong.

fictional not real, written by a writer

1996

BRIDGET JONES'S DIARY

Bridget is invited to a party where she meets Mark Darcy. Unfortunately, Bridget's mother is also there.

I looked around and nearly jumped. There, looking at us, was Mark Darcy. He must have heard all the terrible things my mother had said. I opened my mouth to say something... but he walked away.

Later that evening, Mark Darcy finds Bridget in the garden, and surprises her.

'Will you have dinner with me, Bridget?' he said, as if he was angry with me. I stopped and looked at him for a long time. 'Has my mother told you to ask me out?' I said.

Bridget Jones's Diary was very popular around the world – millions of people bought the book! It was made into a film in 2001, with Renée Zellweger, Hugh Grant and Colin Firth.

▶ 20 This story was written by American writer, Jeff Kinney, about a "wimpy*" kid called Greg Heffley. In this funny book, Greg tells us about his life at school, his friends and adventures, the good times and the not-so-good times.

Greg tells us from the beginning that he isn't happy writing a diary. He is worried that other boys will laugh at him. He says it was his mum's idea.

September, Tuesday

The only reason I agreed to write this diary is because one day, when I am rich and famous, this book will be useful. I won't have to answer people's boring questions about when I was a kid.

I'll be famous one day, but for now I am still in school...

*wimpy (informal) not strong

Greg's best friend is a boy called Rowley.

Greg and Rowley don't always like each other, and they don't always agree. In this part of the story they are angry with each other – Greg thinks Rowley has stolen one of his ideas.

Greg's story is told in words and pictures

May, Monday

The next thing we know, there is a crowd of kids round us. I've never been in a real fight* before, so I didn't know how I should stand or hold my fists*, or anything. Rowley also didn't know how to fight. He just started dancing around.

fight (here) when two people shout and/or hit each other

fists make your hands small, ready to hit someone

Diary of a Wimpy Kid was first seen online. Jeff Kinney started putting some pages on a website called FunBrain, in 2004. Over the next five years, the pages were looked at more than 20 million times. The book became a bestseller and was made into a film in 2010.

Chapter 7

SAVING DIARIES

National Diary Collections

▶ 21

The Italian National Diary Collection is in the small Italian town of Pieve Santo Stefano. It was started in 1984 by Saverio Tutino, and now has 6,500 diaries and life stories. This collection is open to everyone, so that we can read the diaries and letters that are kept here.

Here you will find diaries of women and men, rich people and poor people, and at all times in their lives. The diaries tell us about the thoughts and ideas of people who are not famous, and who could be forgotten.

Every year, the Italian National Diary Collection holds a competition for the best diary or life story. Each winner tells a very different story.

At the age of 72, Clelia Marchi decided to write down the story of her life, and the place where she lived. This diary was not written on paper, but on old bedsheets*.

Find out more at
www.archiviodiari.org
http://www.thegreatdiaryproject.co.uk/
http://ocp.hul.harvard.edu/ww/

bedsheets you put these on your bed to sleep on

The Great Diary Project*

This is a project to save diaries in the UK. It was started by Irving Finkel, who believes that the writings of all people are interesting and should be saved. The people who write these diaries are not famous. We don't always think that what they wrote was important, but in the future it could be useful. It would be fantastic, for example, if we had a lot of diaries written by people from Shakespeare's time!

Families often don't know what to do with old diaries. In the UK they can now send them to the Great Diary Project.

Harvard University

Harvard University has collected the writing of many different women. Their collection is called Women Working 1800 – 1930, and is about women and their jobs.

Writing and Speaking

1a Answer the questions below. Try to use some of the new words and ideas you have learned in this book.

1 Which diary did you find most interesting? Why?

....

2 Did some of the diaries make you feel sad?

....

3 Did anything surprise you?

....

4 Which diary writer/s would you like to learn more about? Why?

....

5 Which diary writer/s did you *not* like? Why?

....

6 Do you prefer real diaries or fictional diaries?

....

7 Why do you think people keep diaries?

....

8 Do you think writing a diary is a good idea? Why?

....

1b Talk in pairs about your answers. Do you agree with each other?

Vocabulary – Jobs

2a **In this book, there are many words to describe someone's job, or what they do. Look for nineteen of these in the wordsearch below.**

S	S	E	S	T	A	T	E	A	G	E	N	T	J	M
O	C	G	S	T	U	N	T	W	O	M	A	N	O	I
N	I	E	H	C	E	L	E	B	R	I	T	Y	U	N
G	E	N	E	S	E	R	E	B	E	L	B	D	R	E
W	N	I	R	A	R	T	I	S	T	V	U	O	N	R
R	T	U	O	S	O	L	D	I	E	R	S	C	A	S
I	I	S	T	E	A	C	H	E	R	E	K	T	L	L
T	S	N	S	I	N	G	E	R	T	Y	E	O	I	A
E	T	C	L	A	S	S	M	A	T	E	R	R	S	V
R	P	H	O	T	O	G	R	A	P	H	E	R	T	E

2b **Now you can complete this sentence: Over thirty million people have bought Anne Frank's diary, and it is published in .... languages.**

2c **Who are we talking about? Use the words from the wordsearch above to help you.**

1 This person helps you to sell your house ....
2 This person's job is to be famous ....
3 This person does dangerous things in films ....
4 This person studies with you ....
5 This person writes in a newspaper ....
6 This person studies animals/plants/people ....

2d **What is your dream job? Why?**

....

....

Vocabulary – Adjectives

3a What do these adjectives mean? Match each adjective from this book with the correct words on the right.

A foreign	☐ **1** something that only you know
B warm	☐ **2** (here) not easy
C imaginary	☐ **3** written by a writer
D secret	☐ **4** better than and different from
E hard	☐ **5** the opposite of cold
F special	☐ **6** something that comes from another country
G traditional	☐ **7** something (eg ideas and way of life) which goes from the past to the present
H fictional	☐ **8** not real

3b Look at the words in the box. Which word goes best with each adjective? The first one has been done as an example. More than one answer is possible.

clothes friend ~~language~~ person
room story welcome work

A foreign ....*language*........
B warm ....
C imaginary ....
D secret ....
E hard ....
F special ....
G traditional ....
H fictional ....

3c Now write sentences using three of the adjectives in 3b.

Reading Comprehension

4 **Who is it? Complete these sentences with people from this book.**

a Musicians' Diaries

Kurt Cobain	Bob Dylan	Heidi Kole

1 .... wrote songs about segregation in 60s America.

2 .... plays music in the subways of New York.

3 .... found being famous difficult, and died when he was young.

b Artists' Pages

Salvador Dalí	Frida Kahlo	Andy Warhol

1 .... painted many pictures of herself, using a lot of colours.

2 .... thought he was very clever, and a fantastic artist.

3 .... loved being with famous people.

c True Stories

Zlata Filipović	Anne Frank	The Freedom Writers
Clelia Marchi	Adam Francis Plummer	

1 .... never lost hope, and believed people were good at heart.

2 .... was not free, and had to learn to write in secret.

3 .... used a diary to help her during the war in Sarajevo.

4 .... used writing to help them change their own lives.

5 .... wrote her life story on old bedsheets.

Key-style activity - Vocabulary

5 Read the sentences about some of the diaries below. Then decide which word (A, B or C) is the best one to complete the sentence.

1 In *Chronicles*, we learn how much Bob Dylan .... being famous.

A wanted **B** hated **C** talked

2 Heidi Kole had ... because the police wanted her to stop playing.

A reasons **B** mistakes **C** problems

3 Anne Frank said, "I see terrible things happening in this world, but when I look up at the sky, I feel ... will be better one day."

A everyone **B** everything **C** nothing

4 Che Guevara says, "All this travelling through 'our' America, has ... me more than I thought."

A bored **B** cost **C** changed

5 David Byrne felt free and happy as he cycled ... many of the world's big cities.

A around **B** back **C** under

6 Put the correct word from the box into the sentences below. The first one has been done as an example.

at	during	from	for	~~into~~	of	out of	with

1 Fishing lines were put ....*into*.... the water, and the men caught a lot of big fish.

2 The birds are not afraid .... us, they have never seen men before.

3 I slept, and didn't wake until Mummy called me .... 5.30.

4 Adam Francis Plummer tells us his wife stayed away .... a short time.

5 Families often don't know what to do .... old diaries.

6 Bob Dylan first became famous .... the 60s.

7 I looked .... the window, and saw Mummy on the bridge!

8 I quickly took a flash bulb .... a photographer.

7 Choose the correct word or phrase in the sentences below.

1 From what I have seen in my years underground, we are probably the *happiest/unhappiest* workers in New York City.

2 Bob Dylan wants to write songs that are *bigger/smaller* than life.

3 Kurt Cobain thought that people *understood/didn't understand* him.

4 This book is special, because it is the *first/last* diary written by a genius.

5 I have learned *something/nothing* from everyone I have met.

6 'I don't suppose *anything/something* will happen with my book,' said Louisa.

7 Perhaps this is the start of another *good/bad* time for my writing.

8 Guevara believed *peace/war* was the best way to change the world.

8 Put each verb in the correct form and tense. The first one has been done as an example.

This is a project **1** ....*to save*...... (save) diaries in the UK. It was **2** .... (start) by Irving Finkel, who **3** .... (believe) that the writings of all people are interesting and should **4** .... (be) saved. The people who **5** .... (write) these diaries are not famous; their diaries don't always seem important at the time, but in the future they could **6** .... (be) useful. It would be fantastic if we **7** .... (have) a lot of diaries **8** .... (write) by people from Shakespeare's time!

Speaking

9a What do you think about these sentences? Tick if you agree (A), disagree (D) or don't know (DK).

	A	D	DK
1 I am only interested in the diaries of famous people.	☐	☐	☐
2 It is important for us to keep the diaries of people who aren't famous.	☐	☐	☐
3 Reading someone's diary helps us to understand who they are.	☐	☐	☐
4 I don't want anyone to read my diary!	☐	☐	☐
5 I don't like reading other people's diaries. I don't want to know their secrets!	☐	☐	☐
6 The diaries of famous people are not true. They know people will read their diaries one day.	☐	☐	☐
7 I keep a diary, or plan to in the future.	☐	☐	☐
8 Writing or reading a diary can change your life.	☐	☐	☐

9b Discuss your ideas in groups. Do you agree with each other?

Writing

10 Write your own diary in English for a week. This will really help you improve your English!

Monday ....

Tuesday ....

Wednesday ....

Thursday ....

Friday ....

Saturday ....

Sunday ....

Syllabus

Prepositions
Location: to, on, inside, at (home), etc.
Time: at, on, in, during, etc.
Direction: to, into, out of, from, etc.
Instrument: by, with

Connectives
and, but, or, when, where, because, if

Verbs
Regular and irregular forms

Verb tenses
Present simple: states, habits, systems and processes (and verbs not used in the continuous form)
Present continuous: present actions
Present perfect simple: indefinite past with never, unfinished past with for
Past Simple: past events
Future with will: offers, promises, predictions, etc.

Verb forms and patterns
Affirmative, interrogative, negative
Infinitives (with and without to) after verbs and adjectives
Regular and common irregular verbs
Passive forms: Present Simple and Past simple with very common verbs (e.g. made, called, born)
Gerunds (verb + -ing) after verbs and prepositions
Gerunds as subjects and objects
Passive forms: present and past simple

Modal verbs
Can: ability, requests, permission
Could: ability
Would: polite requests
Will: future reference, offers, promises, predictions
Should: advice
Must: obligation
Have (got) to: obligation
Need: necessity

Types of clause
Main clause
Co-ordinate clause
Subordinate clause following know, think, believe, say, tell, if, where, when, because
Subordinate clause with if (zero and 1st conditionals)
Defining relative clauses with who, where

Teen ELI Readers

Stage 1
Maureen Simpson, *In Search of a Missing Friend*
Charles Dickens, *Oliver Twist*
Geoffrey Chaucer, *The Canterbury Tales*
Janet Borsbey & Ruth Swan, *The Boat Race Mystery*
Lucy Maud Montgomery, *Anne of Green Gables*
Mark Twain, *A Connecticut Yankee in King Arthur's Court*
Mark Twain, *The Adventures of Huckleberry Finn*
Angela Tomkinson, *Great Friends!*
Edith Nesbit, *The Railway Children*
Eleanor H. Porter, *Pollyanna*
Anna Sewell, *Black Beauty*
Kenneth Grahame, *The Wind in the Willows*

Stage 2
Elizabeth Ferretti, *Dear Diary...*
Angela Tomkinson, *Loving London*
Mark Twain, *The Adventures of Tom Sawyer*
Mary Flagan, *The Egyptian Souvenir*
Maria Luisa Banfi, *A Faraway World*
Frances Hodgson Burnett, *The Secret Garden*
Robert Louis Stevenson, *Treasure Island*
Elizabeth Ferretti, *Adventure at Haydon Point*
William Shakespeare, *The Tempest*
Angela Tomkinson, *Enjoy New York*
Frances Hodgson Burnett, *Little Lord Fauntleroy*
Michael Lacey Freeman, *Egghead*
Michael Lacey Freeman, *Dot to Dot*
Silvana Sardi, *The Boy with the Red Balloon*
Silvana Sardi, *Scotland is Magic!*
Silvana Sardi, *Garpur: My Iceland*
Silvana Sardi, *Follow your Dreams*
Gabriele Rebagliati, *Naoko: my Japan*

Stage 3
Anna Claudia Ramos, *Expedition Brazil*
Charles Dickens, *David Copperfield*
Mary Flagan, *Val's Diary*
Maureen Simpson, *Destination Karminia*
Anonymous, *Robin Hood*
Jack London, *The Call of the Wild*
Louisa May Alcott, *Little Women*
Gordon Gamlin, *Allan: My Vancouver*